The Giant on Windy Hill

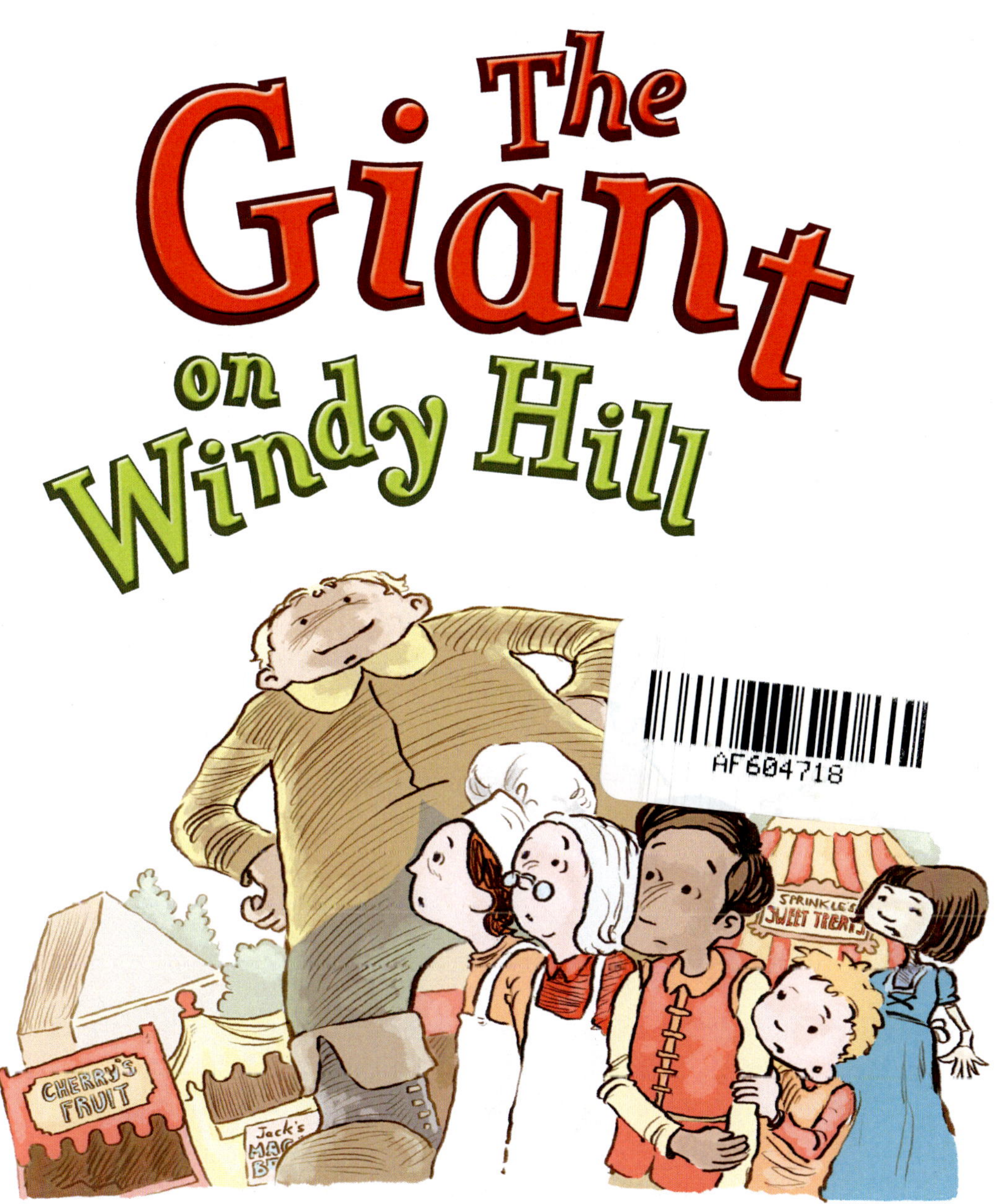

A play by Jill McDougall

Illustrated by Jon Davis

Characters

Giant

Sprinkle

Jack

Cherry

Crumb

Narrator: Every Saturday, people sell their goods at the town market.

Sprinkle: I'm Sprinkle and I sell cakes.

Crumb: I'm Crumb and I sell bread.

Cherry: I'm Cherry and I sell fruit.

Jack: I'm Jack and I sell beans. Magic beans!

Narrator: One day, the market sellers hear a loud thumping.

Sprinkle: It's coming from Windy Hill.

Jack: It sounds like rolling thunder.

Cherry: It's getting closer and CLOSER!

Crumb: It's … It's …

All four: A HUGE GIANT!

The giant stomps into the market.

Narrator: The giant has fists as large as rocks and boots as big as tables.

Giant: Hee! Hee! What do I see?
Lots of goodies just for me!

Sprinkle: The giant is eating my cakes!

Crumb: He's chomping on my bread!

Cherry: He's gobbling up my apples!

Jack: It's lucky I hid my magic beans.

Narrator: Before long, all the cakes, bread and apples are gone.

Giant: Yum! Yum! I've filled my tum,
I've eaten every single crumb.

Giant: Ho! Ho! It's time to go,
But I'll be back again, you know!

The giant leaves.

Sprinkle: What a greedy giant!

Crumb: He said he'd be back!

Cherry: Oh no! What will we do?

Crumb: I know! We could make extra food just for him.

Sprinkle: But then he will **keep** coming back.

Cherry: Perhaps we should stop selling our goods at the market?

Jack: No way! We can't let the giant win.

Narrator: The next market day, the sellers come up with a plan.

Sprinkle: We will stand up to the greedy giant.

Crumb: We will tell him we do not like him taking all our food.

Cherry: And we want him to stop.

Jack: Who will give him the news?

Sprinkle points at Crumb.

Sprinkle: Not me! Crumb will do it!

Crumb points at Cherry.

Crumb: Not a chance! Cherry will do it!

Cherry points at Jack.

Cherry: No way! Jack will do it!

Jack points at himself.

Jack: Me? Are you joking?

Sprinkle: Then we will have to do it together.

RINKLE'S
ET TREATS

Narrator: The sellers decide what they are going to say before the giant arrives. Then they practise.

Sprinkle: Okay. Let's all say it together.

All four: Mr Giant, please go away.

Crumb: Oh, dear! We sound as weak as kittens.

Cherry: We need to sound as brave as lions.

Jack: Let's try again. Repeat after me, "Mr Giant, you must stop eating our food!"

All four: MR GIANT, YOU MUST STOP EATING OUR FOOD!

Jack: That's better. Now we sound as strong as an elephant. Let's practise a few more times.

All four: MR GIANT, YOU MUST STOP EATING OUR FOOD!

Narrator: No one hears the giant tiptoeing towards them.

All four: MR GIANT, YOU MUST STOP EATING OUR FOOD!!

Giant: Hey? Hey? What did you say?

Narrator: The sellers get a terrible fright, but Sprinkle speaks up.

Sprinkle: Mr Giant, we want you to stop eating our food.

Crumb: You are spoiling our market!

Jack: And that makes us sad.

Giant: Sad? Sad? That's too bad!
You have made me really mad!

Narrator: The giant gobbles up everything and walks away.

Sprinkle: Our plan didn't work. It's hopeless!

Crumb: We must not give up! We have to think of something else.

Jack: I have an idea! Listen!

Narrator: Jack whispers his plan to the others.

Cherry: What a great idea!

Narrator: Soon the sellers collect everything they need.

Sprinkle: Here is some sand to sprinkle on the cakes.

Crumb: Here is some mud to bake in the bread.

Cherry: And here is some pepper to put on the fruit.

Jack: The giant is in for a real surprise!

Narrator: The next market day, the giant stomps into the market.

Jack: Here he comes! Get ready, everyone!

Sprinkle: Get your cakes here! Fresh cakes for sale!

Crumb: Get your rye bread here! It's on special today!

Cherry: Get your fruit here! Everything is extra tasty!

Giant: Mmm! Mmm! Lots to eat!
I will munch on every treat.

Narrator: The giant grabs all the cakes, bread and fruit, and starts munching.

Giant: Yum! Yum! ... **Yuck**! **Yuck**!
This food tastes like MUCK!

Narrator: The giant is so angry, his eyes are flashing like fireworks.

Jack: Look out, everyone!

Sprinkle: The giant is stomping on everything!

Crumb: He's making a great big mess!

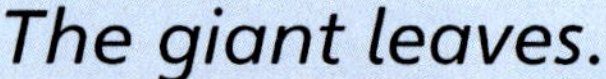

The giant leaves.

Cherry: We must get rid of that terrible giant!

Sprinkle: But **how?**

Narrator: Suddenly, the sellers hear a terrible sound coming from Windy Hill.

Jack: Listen! What's that awful noise?

Sprinkle: It sounds like the wind wailing!

Crumb: Or a stable of donkeys braying!

Cherry: Or … one sad giant crying!

The sellers set off for Windy Hill.

Giant: Sob! Sob! Moan! Moan!
I want to go home and not be alone!

Sprinkle: Mr Giant, what do you mean?

Giant: My home is in the clouds, you see,
Just above your town.
A beanstalk led from here to there,
But someone cut it down!

Jack: Sorry, I did it. I wanted the magic beans that were growing at the top. I did not mean to keep you from your home.

Cherry: I know! We could grow a new beanstalk using one of Jack's magic beans.

Giant: Yes! Yes! Thank you! Yes! And I will help clean up that market mess.

They all set off for the market.

Narrator: The giant helps fix the market and Jack grows a beanstalk using one of his magic beans. Then it is time for the giant to go home.

All four: Goodbye, Mr Giant!

Giant: Ho! Ho! Hee! Hee!
Thank you, friends, for helping me.